Francis Frith's
Warrington

JANICE HAYES has worked at Warrington Museum for 25 years, researching the town's history and helping communities to record their past. She has been particularly involved with the Museum's extensive photographic archive and is delighted to have been asked to work with the Francis Frith collection.
A native of Warrington Janice enjoys helping others to reminisce and rediscover the town's historic landmarks.
'Francis Frith's Around Warrington' is her sixth publication, commemorating the Golden Jubilee year through many fascinating images of the town in the early 1950s, at the beginning of Queen Elizabeth II's reign.

Photographic Memories

Francis Frith's
Warrington

Janice Hayes

FRITH BOOK Co

First published in the United Kingdom in 2002 by
Frith Book Company Ltd

Paperback Edition 2002
ISBN 1-85937-507-3

British Library Cataloguing in Publication Data

Francis Frith's Warrington
Janice Hayes

Frith Book Company Ltd
Frith's Barn, Teffont,
Salisbury, Wiltshire SP3 5QP
Tel: +44 (0) 1722 716 376
Email: info@francisfrith.co.uk
www.francisfrith.co.uk

Printed and bound in Great Britain

Front Cover: Warrington, Bridge Street c1955 W29060

Contents

Francis Frith: *Victorian Pioneer*

FRANCIS FRITH, Victorian founder of the world-famous photographic archive, was a complex and multi-talented man. A devout Quaker and a highly successful Victorian businessman, he was both philosophic by nature and pioneering in outlook.

By 1855 Francis Frith had already established a wholesale grocery business in Liverpool, and sold it for the astonishing sum of £200,000, which is the equivalent today of over £15,000,000. Now a multi-millionaire, he was able to indulge his passion for travel. As a child he had pored over travel books written by early explorers, and his fancy and imagination had been stirred by family holidays to the sublime mountain regions of Wales and Scotland. 'What a land of spirit-stirring and enriching scenes and places!' he had written. He was to return to these scenes of grandeur in later years to 'recapture the thousands of vivid and tender memories', but with a different purpose. Now in his thirties, and captivated by the new science of photography, Frith set out on a series of pioneering journeys to the Nile regions that occupied him from 1856 until 1860.

Intrigue and Adventure

He took with him on his travels a specially-designed wicker carriage that acted as both dark-room and sleeping chamber. These far-flung journeys were packed with intrigue and adventure. In his life story, written when he was sixty-three, Frith tells of being held captive by bandits, and of fighting 'an awful midnight battle to the very point of surrender with a deadly pack of hungry, wild dogs'. Sporting flowing Arab costume, Frith arrived at Akaba by camel seventy years before Lawrence, where he encountered 'desert princes and rival sheikhs, blazing with jewel-hilted swords'.

During these extraordinary adventures he was assiduously exploring the desert regions bordering the Nile and patiently recording the antiquities and peoples with his camera. He was the first photographer to venture beyond the sixth cataract. Africa was still the mysterious 'Dark Continent', and Stanley and Livingstone's historic meeting was a decade into the future. The conditions for picture taking confound belief. He laboured for hours in his wicker dark-room in the sweltering heat of the desert, while the volatile chemicals fizzed dangerously in their trays. Often he was forced to work in remote tombs and caves where conditions were cooler. Back in London he exhibited his photographs and was 'rapturously cheered' by members of the Royal Society. His reputation as a photographer was made overnight. An eminent modern historian has likened their impact on the population of the time to that on our own generation of the first photographs taken on the surface of the moon.

Venture of a Life-Time

Characteristically, Frith quickly spotted the opportunity to create a new business as a specialist publisher of photographs. He lived in an era of immense and sometimes violent change. For the poor in the early part of Victoria's reign work was a drudge and the hours long, and people had precious little free time to enjoy themselves. Most had no transport other than a cart or gig at their disposal, and had not travelled far beyond the boundaries of their own town or village. However,

by the 1870s, the railways had threaded their way across the country, and Bank Holidays and half-day Saturdays had been made obligatory by Act of Parliament. All of a sudden the ordinary working man and his family were able to enjoy days out and see a little more of the world.

With characteristic business acumen, Francis Frith foresaw that these new tourists would enjoy having souvenirs to commemorate their days out. In 1860 he married Mary Ann Rosling and set out with the intention of photographing every city, town and village in Britain. For the next thirty years he travelled the country by train and by pony and trap, producing fine photographs of seaside resorts and beauty spots that were keenly bought by millions of Victorians. These prints were painstakingly pasted into family albums and pored over during the dark nights of winter, rekindling precious memories of summer excursions.

The Rise of Frith & Co

Frith's studio was soon supplying retail shops all over the country. To meet the demand he gathered about him a small team of photographers, and published the work of independent artist-photographers of the calibre of Roger Fenton and Francis Bedford. In order to gain some understanding of the scale of Frith's business one only has to look at the catalogue issued by Frith & Co in 1886: it runs to some 670 pages, listing not only many thousands of views of the British Isles but also many photographs of most European countries, and China, Japan, the USA and Canada – note the sample page shown above from the hand-written *Frith & Co* ledgers detailing pictures taken. By 1890 Frith had created the greatest specialist photographic publishing company in the world,

Frith's death, a new card measuring 5.5 x 3.5 inches became the standard format, but it was not until 1902 that the divided back came into being, with address and message on one face and a full-size illustration on the other. *Frith & Co* were in the vanguard of postcard development, and Frith's sons Eustace and Cyril continued their father's monumental task, expanding the number of views offered to the public and recording more and more places in Britain, as the coasts and countryside were opened up to mass travel.

Francis Frith died in 1898 at his villa in Cannes, his great project still growing. The archive he created continued in business for another seventy years. By 1970 it contained over a third of a million pictures of 7,000 cities, towns and villages. The massive photographic record Frith has left to us stands as a living monument to a special and very remarkable man.

with over 2,000 outlets – more than the combined number that Boots and W H Smith have today! The picture on the right shows the *Frith & Co* display board at Ingleton in the Yorkshire Dales. Beautifully constructed with mahogany frame and gilt inserts, it could display up to a dozen local scenes.

Postcard Bonanza

The ever-popular holiday postcard we know today took many years to develop. In 1870 the Post Office issued the first plain cards, with a pre-printed stamp on one face. In 1894 they allowed other publishers' cards to be sent through the mail with an attached adhesive halfpenny stamp. Demand grew rapidly, and in 1895 a new size of postcard was permitted called the court card, but there was little room for illustration. In 1899, a year after

Frith's Archive: *A Unique Legacy*

FRANCIS FRITH'S legacy to us today is of immense significance and value, for the magnificent archive of evocative photographs he created provides a unique record of change in 7,000 cities, towns and villages throughout Britain over a century and more. Frith and his fellow studio photographers revisited locations many times down the years to update their views, compiling for us an enthralling and colourful pageant of British life and character.

We tend to think of Frith's sepia views of Britain as nostalgic, for most of us use them to conjure up memories of places in our own lives with which we have family associations. It often makes us forget that to Francis Frith they were records of daily life as it was actually being lived in the cities, towns and villages of his day. The Victorian age was one of great and often bewildering change for ordinary people, and though the pictures evoke an impression of slower times, life was as busy and hectic as it is today.

We are fortunate that Frith was a photographer of the people, dedicated to recording the minutiae of everyday life. For it is this sheer wealth of visual data, the painstaking chronicle of changes in dress, transport, street layouts, buildings, housing, engineering and landscape that captivates us so much today. His remarkable images offer us a powerful link with the past and with the lives of our ancestors.

Today's Technology

Computers have now made it possible for Frith's many thousands of images to be accessed almost instantly. In the Frith archive today, each photograph is carefully 'digitised' then stored on a CD Rom. Frith archivists can locate a single photograph amongst thousands within seconds. Views can be catalogued and sorted under a variety of categories of place and content to the immediate benefit of researchers.

Inexpensive reference prints can be created for them at the touch of a mouse button, and a wide range of books and other printed materials assembled and published for a wider, more general readership - in the next twelve months over a hundred Frith local history titles will be published! The day-to-day workings of the archive are very different from how they were in Francis Frith's time: imagine the herculean task of sorting through eleven tons of glass negatives as Frith had to do to locate a particular sequence of pictures! Yet

See Frith at www.francisfrith.co.uk

the archive still prides itself on maintaining the same high standards of excellence laid down by Francis Frith, including the painstaking cataloguing and indexing of every view.

It is curious to reflect on how the internet now allows researchers in America and elsewhere greater instant access to the archive than Frith himself ever enjoyed. Many thousands of individual views can be called up on screen within seconds on one of the Frith internet sites, enabling people living continents away to revisit the streets of their ancestral home town, or view places in Britain where they have enjoyed holidays. Many overseas researchers welcome the chance to view special theme selections, such as transport, sports, costume and ancient monuments.

We are certain that Francis Frith would have heartily approved of these modern developments in imaging techniques, for he himself was always working at the very limits of Victorian photographic technology.

The Value of the Archive Today

Because of the benefits brought by the computer, Frith's images are increasingly studied by social historians, by researchers into genealogy and ancestory, by architects, town planners, and by teachers and schoolchildren involved in local history projects.

In addition, the archive offers every one of us an opportunity to examine the places where we and our families have lived and worked down the years. Highly successful in Frith's own era, the archive is now, a century and more on, entering a new phase of popularity.

The Past in Tune with the Future

Historians consider the Francis Frith Collection to be of prime national importance. It is the only archive of its kind remaining in private ownership and has been valued at a million pounds. However, this figure is now rapidly increasing as digital technology enables more and more people around the world to enjoy its benefits.

Francis Frith's archive is now housed in an historic timber barn in the beautiful village of Teffont in Wiltshire. Its founder would not recognize the archive office as it is today. In place of the many thousands of dusty boxes containing glass plate negatives and an all-pervading odour of photographic chemicals, there are now ranks of computer screens. He would be amazed to watch his images travelling round the world at unimaginable speeds through network and internet lines.

The archive's future is both bright and exciting. Francis Frith, with his unshakeable belief in making photographs available to the greatest number of people, would undoubtedly approve of what is being done today with his lifetime's work. His photographs, depicting our shared past, are now bringing pleasure and enlightenment to millions around the world a century and more after his death.

Warrington - *An Introduction*

FRANCIS FRITH'S photographer first appeared in Warrington with his cumbersome plate camera in 1894, three years before Queen Victoria's Diamond Jubilee. Children born in the closing years of the 19th century grew up to witness a major redevelopment of Warrington's town centre. Between 1880 and 1915 Bridge Street and Buttermarket Street were widened, and many historic buildings such as the Old Fox Inn disappeared. Warrington Bridge was rebuilt with the expectation that its new 80-foot width would prove more than adequate to the demands of rush hour traffic.

The era of the horse gave way to that of the horseless carriage. First trams and later the motor bus appeared on Warrington's streets, but the age of the private motor car was still a long way off on the horizon. Commercial barges still glided along the

Bridgewater Canal, and ocean-going vessels brought raw materials along the Manchester Ship Canal and exported the products of north-western industries. By the early 20th century, Warrington could claim to be 'the Town of Many Industries'.

In 1947 Warrington celebrated the centenary of its incorporation as a Municipal Borough; a commemorative publication looked back with pride on the changes which had taken place. 'Streets have been paved, widened and properly equipped with sewers; houses and bridges have been built; hospitals, schools, parks, baths, a cemetery, and electricity, gas and transport undertakings have been acquired and developed; and the council has borrowed and loaned large sums of money'. The town seemed well-equipped to face the challenges of the post-war world.

In the early 1950s another of Frith's photographers captured Warrington at the dawn of a new Elizabethan age. Local children celebrated Queen Elizabeth's coronation in June 1953, but only a fortunate few watched it on television. They would grow up in a very different world from their Victorian grandparents. Slowly the country emerged from the austerity of World War II and the high street shops were full of consumer goods again.

Bridge Street was still the retail centre of Warrington, with traditional family drapers such as Broadbent & Turner, Lee & Clarke, Hodgkinsons and Hancock and Wood. Demobbed National Servicemen might be clothed at Burton's or the Fifty-Shilling Tailors and shod at the Public Benefit Boot & Shoe Company. Housewives might treat themselves to a permanent wave at Birch Browne's hairdressing salon before buying their groceries. Old-established family firms such as Henry Milling & Co or Peter Leigh and Sons still weighed out tea or sliced ham whilst the customer waited. Singleton's and Gaskell's, the butchers, still supplied the traditional Sunday roast or the breakfast bacon.

Small children watched in fascination whilst the assistants in the Maypole Dairy at Market Gate took a lump of golden butter between a pair of wooden paddles and patted it into a carefully-judged half pound. Then, as an extra treat, the youngsters hopped into Long's sweet shop to consider how much of their sixpence pocket money to spend on

a quarter of satin cushions or a bag of sherbet dip.

Warrington's streets always seem bustling in Frith's 1950s photographs, but wages were still low, and shoppers were prudent with their money. Newly-weds still spent their early married life at their parents' home, and when they did move into their rented council house few cared to risk buying furniture on the 'never-never' or credit.

The journey into town from the new housing estates on the outskirts was made by a Corporation bus, which would drop off its passengers in the main streets, conveniently near to the shops. Pedestrians had to give increasing notice to the through traffic as it circled the roundabout at Market Gate, passing through east-west on the A57 from Manchester to Liverpool or north-south on the busy A49. More private cars were in evidence, but they were still an expensive luxury in the 1950s, and a rare sight even in the outlying villages of Lymm, Thelwall and Moore. By the time of Frith's return visit in the 1960s, the Wilderspool Bridge was improving traffic flow on the A49, but the constant closure of the swing bridges over the Ship Canal was proving a growing source of irritation to rush-hour travellers.

The Frith views of the 1950s and 1960s record a Warrington in limbo. Outwardly little changed from the pre-war years, with Sankey Street and the Old Market area waiting to be redeveloped. Ambitious plans had been prepared in the 1930s, but they were shelved during World War II. Planners and

conservationists debated the rival claims of traffic, people and historic buildings. There were wider issues to be considered, such as the fate of acres of derelict World War II installations at the former Padgate RAF camp and the Risley munitions factory. The long-term future of the Burtonwood airbase was also uncertain, representing further development opportunities. Warrington had the potential to become a key regional growth point - or possibly find itself merely an overspill town for Greater Manchester.

If Frith's photographer had re-appeared at Queen Elizabeth's Silver Jubilee in 1977, he would have found Warrington in a massive transition. The town had been granted New Town status in 1968, and the Master Plan for Warrington's New Town proposed to create 'a prosperous dynamic town of opportunity and innovation'. The New Town Development Corporation was to develop new districts at Padgate, Birchwood and Westbrook; each was to have an infra-structure of roads, employment sites, shopping centres, housing, schools and community facilities. Other traditional villages, such as Lymm, Thelwall, Grappenhall and Moore, were largely unaffected by the proposals, and maintained much of their rural character.

Warrington Borough Council gave priority to regenerating the Old Market Area in partnership with private developers. Although the scale of the redevelopment meant the disappearance of a number of historic buildings, the 16th-century Barley Mow Inn found itself swathed in a protective cocoon to emerge as the focal point for Golden Square, which was completed in 1983. The new shopping development attracted new chain stores to the town, and Bridge Street and Market Gate were no longer the centre of retail activity.

The pressure from through traffic was supposed to be eased by the surrounding motorway network and the proposed inner ring roads. The decline of traffic on the Ship Canal should in theory have reduced congestion, but the national trend away from the use of public transport continued to add to Warrington's traffic problems. Shoppers could at least park in the new multi-storey car park at Legh Street, but they would find many of the familiar shops from their childhood had disappeared.

The market had moved to its new site in Bank Street. Most of the family department stores such as Hodgkinsons, Broadbent and Turner, and Lee & Clarke had closed, and only Hancock and Wood had moved with the times. Millings and Peter Leigh's, the grocers, along with the butchers, the bakers and even the ironmongers, were rapidly giving way to supermarkets. Eating habits were changing as foreign foods sampled on cheap package holidays found favour over traditional fare, and working wives had no time to wait for their goods to be weighed out.

A digital image bank of Warrington in the Golden Jubilee year of 2002 would reveal the pace of change over the last twenty-five years. Warrington now promotes itself as the 'Town where Business Goes to Work'. Many of the town's traditional industries have disappeared, a reflection of the national decline in manufacturing. Rationalisation in the wire, iron and steel industries in the 1980s brought major changes to the old thoroughfare of Church Street. The site of Ryland's wireworks became available for redevelopment; it was acquired by Sainsbury's supermarket, which was looking to expand its operation in the north. As cotton mills closed all over the country in the face of foreign competition, the former Cockhedge Mill became redundant, whilst the retail trade was booming. Planners frowned on industry close to the town centre, and the development of the Cockhedge Shopping Centre was an ideal solution.

Traffic congestion frequently sees rush-hour Warrington gridlocked, particularly when the overstretched motorway network is closed by an accident. The town's main streets are pedestrianised, and have been revamped by a major programme of public artworks. Doubtless in time the controversial 'Skittles' at Market Gate will prove as popular as the old roundabout. New retail developments have been announced for Golden Square and the Market area, which could lead to even more dramatic changes in the townscape. Casually-dressed shoppers throng the chain stores which could be in almost any town's high street, and splash out with their credit cards.

Families enjoy snacks at fast food restaurants, often preferring a vegetarian option; the Sunday roast is a thing of the past, thanks to microwave meals and worries over BSE.

Today's Warrington children are citizens of a global village in an era of mass communications. As they shop with their parents at Sainsbury's supermarket, it is by no means certain that they will recognise the nearby old Grammar School or even the Parish Church. Yet it is comforting to know that despite the pace of change, many of the historic buildings which Frith recorded in the 1890s still exist, and that Warrington has retained its unique character.

Warrington, Bridge Street c1950 W29008

Around the Town Centre

The Bridge and Marshall's Gardens c1960
W29065

Warrington owes its regional and national importance to its role as a crossing point over the River Mersey. There has been a bridge at Warrington since the 13th century, when the town centre began to develop in its present location away from the medieval village off Church Street. This panoramic view shows the elegant single-spanned reinforced concrete bridge constructed between 1911 and 1915. Designed by the Warrington-born engineer John James Webster, the eighty-foot wide bridge was hailed as the most handsome in Britain. King George V opened the first half on 7 July 1913 by remote control from Warrington Town Hall!

▲ **Marshall's Gardens c1960** W29067

It is time to relax in Marshall's Gardens and look over Bridge Foot. To the left, Garlands Garage still has Austin and Wolseley cars for sale, whilst a steamroller rumbles past the Crosville bus stand. In the centre the Tower Restaurant is still standing next to the Old Academy. Across the road, on the corner of Mersey Street, the Packet House Inn hints at the days when packet boats carried passengers along the Mersey to Liverpool. Neon advertising signs telling us that 'Players Please' and 'Senior Service Satisfy' show that smoking had still to become an anti-social pastime.

◄ **St James' Church and Wilderspool Causeway c1965**
W29108

A strangely unfamiliar sight to today's motorists: Wilderspool Causeway is virtually traffic-free. The two parked minis and the Volkswagen car show that this is the era of The Beatles. Next to Marshall's familiar newsagent's shop, James Bennett & Co. are still manufacturing shirts and pyjamas; St James' Church, built in 1829, dominates the scene.

Bridge Foot from Wilderspool Causeway c1960 W29068

A lone vehicle heads towards Warrington town centre down the new Wilderspool Bridge. Opened in May 1957 by Alderman Marshall, the flyover bridge replaced the Wilderspool railway crossing, a bottleneck on the main A49 highway. Bishop's Wharf can be seen behind the half-timbered buildings on Knutsford Road (right). These canal carriers and warehousemen offered a 'regular service between Warrington and Liverpool by fleet of new-built steel barges'. 'Specialists in the handling of hides and tanning materials', they supplied numerous Warrington tanneries, especially at Howley. Today Bishop's Wharf is the site of the Riverside Retail Park, and the tanneries are gone.

Marshall's Gardens c1960 W29072

Sun worshippers in Marshall's Gardens turn their backs on landmarks which will soon disappear. The two towers of Howley Power Station had dominated the landscape since the extensions of 1946, but the site had supplied Warrington's electricity since 1900. To its left is the bulk of Manchester and District Farmers Ltd, who were millers and cattle food dealers.

▼ The War Memorial c1960 W29071

This simple 30-foot high granite obelisk was originally unveiled in November 1925 to commemorate Warrington's servicemen lost in the 1914-18 War. The memorial was appropriately sited at Bridge Foot, the scene of many battles in Warrington's past. To the memorial's right is the half-timbered group of buildings housing the New Bridge Cafe and Marsh's Commercial College.

The Academy and the ▶ Cromwell Statue 1901
47251

With the widening of Bridge Street from the 1880s, the old Warrington Academy was again revealed and preserved. From 1757 until 1762 this had been the earlier site of a higher education institution for Nonconformists, who were barred by law from attending Oxford or Cambridge University. To commemorate the tercentenary of Cromwell's birth in 1899, Councillor Frederick Monks presented this statue by John Bell to the town. Cromwell was also a nonconformist, so this seemed an appropriate site for the statue, particularly since his troops had fought a battle with Scottish Royalists at Warrington Bridge in 1648.

▼ The New Roundabout at Bridge Foot c1960 W29070

The view from the roundabout has changed dramatically since 1960. The Academy building (far left) was sliced from its foundations and moved to the empty plot where the Tower Restaurant stood. After this feat of engineering in May 1981, the Academy was demolished and rebuilt! The single-storey public conveniences (far right) vanished with the building of the second river crossing.

◀ Bridge Street c1950

W29008

This section of Bridge Street has changed drastically since this view towards Market Gate was taken. The wallpaper shop and its neighbours on the right-hand side of the street would be demolished during the construction of Academy Way. Whilst Harris' and the Feathers Inn remain near Friar's Gate, Toft's Bakery between them (left) has closed its doors.

Bridge Street looking towards the Town Centre c1950 W29002
Once, stage coaches thundered through the wide central archway of the Lion Hotel. We can see it centre right in this high-level view, which was taken from Martin's Bank on the corner of Friar's Gate. Times have changed! Now Birch, Browne & Son's Hairdressing Salons (to the Lion's right) offers new-fangled 'Permanent Waving' to its clients!

Bridge Street from the Town Centre c1950 W29001
This view down Bridge Street, looking towards Bridge Foot, shows the impact of the redevelopment of the earlier 20th century. The west side of the street (right) was completely rebuilt between the 1880s and 1908 to create a much wider thoroughfare. The distinctive chequer-board road crossing and chained railings suggest that 1950s pedestrians were finding traffic more of a hazard.

Bridge Street c1955
W29060
The corner of Bridge Street and Buttermarket Street (left) was rebuilt just before the First World War. By 1955 the old-established butchers, Singletons, had given way to Woodhouse's furniture shop. On the opposite side of the road, Boots the chemists were still firmly entrenched on the corner of Sankey Street.

Bridge Street c1950 W29006
Bridge Street was one of four main streets intersecting at Market Gate. All were not only shopping streets,
but a key part of the regional road network. From 1938 to 1966 Market Gate roundabout, seen in the foreground,
attempted to speed the flow of traffic on the A49 and A57 routes through the town centre.

The Circus and Bridge Street c1955 W29034
There's not an elephant in sight at Warrington's Circus! Warringtonians would probably describe this as Market
Gate, but Frith's view records the original concept of 1908 to create four matching corners, 'a spacious circus,
perfectly symmetrical in shape with a ring of singularly graceful buildings'. Piecemeal redevelopment of Market
Gate prevented realisation of this ambitious scheme.

The Circus and Bridge Street c1955 W29062

The banner on Boots' Corner advertising Warrington's annual Walton Horse Show suggests this photograph was taken near Whitsuntide. Meanwhile, shoppers could pop into Longs (left) for unrationed sweets or stand and admire the dexterity of the assistants in the Maypole Dairy next door as they patted a pound of golden butter into shape.

Bridge Street c1955 W29001a

Bridge Street is bustling with Saturday afternoon shoppers. Next to Singleton's the butchers is the Midland Bank's fine facade. The plainer frontage of Roberts' shoe shop is followed by the protruding shop windows of Hancock and Wood, shielded by sun awnings. Next comes the National Provincial Bank (now demolished). The bus on the left passes the distinctive roofline of the Howard building with its tall chimneys and imperious lions, home to Broadbent and Turners, 'General and Furnishing Drapers', and Boydell Bros, the tailors. Further down on the right a bus passes Bradley's Corner and turns into Rylands Street.

Bridge Street c1955
W29021
Bridge Street was clearly Warrington's shopping centre in the 1950s. The west side offered some of Warrington's finest shops. Next to Boots came the old-established drapers Lee & Clarke, then came the Public Benefit Boot & Shoe Co, Gaskell's the butchers, Hallett the jewellers (goldsmiths and silversmiths), Carter's Cafe and finally the awnings of Hodgkinsons, another traditional drapers and house furnishers.

◀ **Market Gate c1965**
W29102
The last days of the corner of Sankey Street and Horsemarket Street are approaching. Trendy Top Pic fashions have moved into Milling's old shop, but Peter Leigh & Son's traditional grocers survive next door. Percival Pearse, Stationers, still occupy a fine 1850s building (left), but all of this corner would soon be demolished to make way for Golden Square.

Bridge Street c1955 W29037
Hancock & Wood and Roberts shoe shop are almost all that remain of this 1955 scene. Henry Milling & Co's family grocers with its familiar Ovaltine sign soon disappeared; Gaskell's Farm Shop stopped selling bacon, and time was running out for John Manners' 'Gents & Boys' clothes shop. Worst still was the loss of Carter's café, which a 1930s guidebook described as 'one of the finest in the South West Lancashire district (with) well appointed Luncheon and Tea Rooms, Ball Room etc', where 'table attendance, setting and quality, all combine to give a sense of taste and refinement'.

Winwick Street c1965 W29099
This view from the Lord Rodney Hotel looking towards Central Station shows the increase in road signs and road markings necessary with the growth of road traffic in the 1960s. Asco, the Accessories Supply Co, and the neighbouring shops on the left (now demolished) stood on the corner of Pinners Brow, a street name recording Warrington's former pin-making industry.

The Circus and Sankey Street c1955

W29036

Road traffic was much lighter in the 1950s, but even then Sankey Street represented a major bottleneck on the main A57 Liverpool to Manchester Road. Below the Town Clock the blackened sandstone of Holy Trinity Church bears witness to the effects of industrial pollution. Meanwhile a rag and bone man trots on his way in front of the Metro Cleaners.

Horsemarket Street c1955 W29009
Warrington did once have a horsemarket, but it was further down the road, along Winwick Street outside Central Station. The last horsefair took place just before the First World War, long before this photograph was taken. Here, shopping expedition completed, mother and son walk down Horsemarket Street, passing Sterlings shoe shop on the corner of Lyme Street (right.) Perhaps she has just called in at the Fifty Shilling Tailors on the other side of the road, next to H Samuel's the jewellers. Notice how formally dressed everyone looks in the 1950s, compared with today's casual shoppers!

The Barley Mow Inn
c1950 W29014
Built in 1561 in the reign of Queen Elizabeth I, the half-timbered Barley Mow Inn is the one constant factor in Warrington's old Market Place. The figure seated on the corner of Market Street is probably Charlie Lee, a well-known stallholder at the fish market opposite. Perhaps he is composing his latest daily poem to amuse his customers.

Ye Olde Barley Mow c1955 W29058

'Beer drawn from cellars centuries old', proclaims the sign over the tunnel entrance which led into the old General Market behind. The Vine Tavern competes for trade on the corner of Market Street and Lyme Street to the right. The wool shop to the left occupied the former offices of William Beamont, Warrington's first mayor in 1847.

Sankey Street c1955 W29046

Warston Pictures proudly presents 'My Six Convicts' at its Cameo Cinema on the corner of Springfield Street, opposite Bank House (right.) In the distance Eustance's clock is almost calling time on an area of Sankey Street which was under threat of demolition. The section from the white gable end was later remodelled in the development of Golden Square.

The Town Hall and the New Gates 1895

36688

Warrington's Town Hall was originally Bank Hall, built between 1749-50 by the world-famous architect James Gibbs as a home for a local businessman, Thomas Patten. Gibbs had previously designed St Martin in the Fields church in London and the Radcliffe Library in Oxford, whilst Patten's wealth came from his copper works at Bank Quay. The building was bought from the family to become Warrington's Town Hall in 1872. The ornate gates replaced the brick wall which the Pattens had erected in Sankey Street to give them privacy from curious passers-by. Warrington's ratepayers demanded the right to see their new seat of government!

▼ **The Town Hall Gates 1901** 47247

Councillor Frederick Monks of the Monks Hall Iron Foundry presented the Town Hall Gates to Warrington on Walking Day, 28 June 1895. Originally designed by the Coalbrookdale Iron Company for Sandringham House, and shown at the International Exhibition of 1862, they were adapted by replacing the central Prince of Wales' feathers with the Warrington coat of arms.

▼ **The Park Gates and the Town Hall c1955** W29022

Can you spot the difference? The Walker fountain was demolished for scrap metal as a patriotic wartime gesture in March 1942. Two identical versions of the fountain still survive in a Glasgow park and Pretoria city zoo in South Africa! The Town Hall gates have since been decorated in their royal colours to celebrate Queen Elizabeth's Silver Jubilee of 1977.

◀ **The Town Hall and the Fountain 1901** 47249

This ornate green and gold-painted cast iron fountain was presented to the town in May 1900 in honour of Peter Walker, founder of Walker's Brewery. Manufactured by Walter Mcfarlane & Company of Possil Park, Glasgow, it cost the princely sum of £1,000. On the 40-foot ground basin were four seated figures representing art, science, literature and commerce. Above their heads were twelve panels depicting the signs of the zodiac. Higher still on the upper basin were eight sea urchins blowing their horns, and finally the pinnacle was composed of four entwined dolphins.

◀ **Bank Park Gardens c1965** W29113
A view from the Town Hall driveway towards Sankey Street shows the typical flowerbeds of a municipal park. The trees on the far left hide Bank House, home of the railway pioneer William Allcard, who worked with George Stephenson on the Liverpool to Manchester railway. Allcard lived at Bank House from 1839 to 1854, and served as Warrington's second mayor in 1848.

◄ **Queen's Gardens 1901**
47248
The former private gardens of the residents of Palmyra Square were purchased in 1897 as a park to celebrate Queen Victoria's Diamond Jubilee, and were opened to the public on the 17th of October 1898. The original Bold Street Methodist Chapel, built in 1849-50, can be seen in the middle background.

◄ The Bowling Green Bank Park c1955 W29045

Bank Park was fashioned out of the private gardens of Bank Hall. Opened to the public in 1873, it was the only source of recreation for working-class families living in the crowded town centre courtyards. By 1900, adults could stroll in the fresh air and listen to a band, whilst children enjoyed the delights of an aviary and an aquarium.

▼ Queen's Gardens c1955 W29047

Sun-worshippers contemplate two memorials in Queen's Gardens. On the left is a fountain commemorating Queen Victoria, and on the right is a monument to Warrington soldiers of the Queen's Lancashire Regiment killed in the Boer War. Unveiled in 1907, Alfred Drury's bronze statue features Lt Colonel MacCarthay O'Leary, killed leading the charge at Pieter's Hill during the relief of Ladysmith.

◄ Queen's Gardens c1955 W29049

This view from Springfield Street shows the newly-laid-out flowerbeds of the revamped gardens. The tower in the background belongs to the CWS printing works (formerly Garnett's cabinet works) behind Woolworth's shop in Sankey Street.

The Town Centre and Buttermarket Street c1950 W29005
Frith's intrepid photographer sought a high vantage point at Boots Corner for this view down Buttermarket Street.
This was still the main A57 route to Manchester, and the terminus for several local bus routes. The Scotland Road
area can be seen in the distance - this was at a time before the impact of the building of the Cockhedge Shopping
Centre in the 1980s.

The Town Centre from Boots Corner c1955 W29025
Burton's the tailors displays its fine facade with Portland stone columns, which was created by rebuilding the corner of Horsemarket Street and Buttermarket Street in 1937. Buttermarket Street was the favourite haunt of GIs from Burtonwood airbase: they would drink at the Pelican Inn (to Burton's right), dance at the Casino Club above, go to the movies, or play billiards at the domed Empire building.

Church Street 1894 33805
Oliver Cromwell did not sleep here! However, popular history associates these Tudor cottages on the corner of Eldon Street with Cromwell's visit to Warrington in 1648 whilst pursuing the Scottish army. He actually lodged next door at the Spotted Leopard Inn (later the General Wolfe pub.) At the time of this photograph, Mason's Stores were selling herb beer from one of the cottages!

Buttermarket Street 1894 33806
By 1894, the Old Fox Inn had closed its doors in the face of competition from the newer Crown and Sceptre Inn to its left. A variety of tenants succeeded Beswick, including Charlie Lee's oyster shop and Lewis' Old Curiosity Shop, before demolition threatened in 1912 with the widening of Buttermarket Street. In an attempt to preserve the 17th-century building, its timbers were carefully numbered and it was dismantled for re-assembly on a new site. The grandiose scheme came to nothing as the First World War intervened, and the remains of the Old Fox lay rotting in Victoria Park.

The Parish Church 1894 33797
Although a church dedicated to St Elphin is recorded in the Domesday Book of 1086, there had probably been a place of worship here from the 7th century. The site of the Parish Church was a natural centre for a settlement, on raised ground overlooking the ancient ford over the Mersey. By the early 13th century it stood at the heart of the medieval village of Warrington, and adjoining the lord of the manor's castle. Much of the present building dates from Victorian reconstruction work commissioned by Rector William Quekett between 1858-62.

The Parish Church c1955 W29041

St Elphin's crowning glory is its spire, soaring over the landscape at a height of about 281 feet, making it the third highest parish church spire in England. The Rev Quekett knew the value of a good slogan, and launched an appeal for 'a guinea for a golden cock!' His fundraising technique was successful, and the spire's weathercock is gilded with sovereigns.

▼ **The Parish Church, the Interior looking East 1895** 36691

The parish church interior enshrines much of Warrington's history through its memorials. An effigy of Lord Winmarleigh, great-grandson of the builder of Warrington's Town Hall, can be seen in St Anne's Chapel on the right. Hidden away on the left is the Boteler Chapel, containing several family tombs, including that of Sir Thomas Boteler, founder of the Grammar School.

▼ **The Training College Chapel 1894** 33801

St Katherine's Chapel was part of the complex which formed Warrington Teachers' Training College. In the early hours of 28 December 1923 a devastating fire swept through the main buildings beside the Parish Church, and by daylight only a blackened shell remained. The chapel survived, and later became a community centre in the new housing estate at St Katherine's Way.

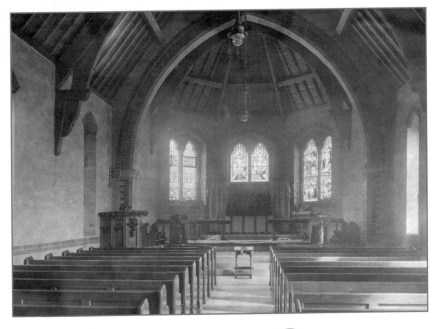

▲ **St Mary's Catholic Church, the Interior 1895** 36694

St Mary's Church was built between 1875-77 on the site of a former cotton factory in Buttermarket Street, close to the working-class districts which provided its congregation. Designed by the famous Pugin family of architects, its ornate interior added in the 1880s has found favour with architectural historians. The church was completed in 1906 by the addition of a tower.

The Grammar School 1895 36690

Sir Thomas Boteler, lord of the manor of Warrington, left provision in his will of 1526 to establish a school 'whereby men's sons might learn grammar to the intent that they might learn to know Almighty God'. The Boteler Grammar School was built in Bag Lane, off Church Street, on the outskirts of the medieval village of Warrington.

The Grammar School 1895   36689
This view will be familiar to users of Sainsbury's petrol station today! The old premises on School Brow had been rebuilt in 1863; but as pupil numbers grew, and Rylands' Wireworks encroached on the site, land for a new school in Latchford was bought in 1924. The new building in Grammar School Road opened in September 1940.

The Suspension Bridge and the Parish Church c1955   W29055
Howley is one of Warrington's oldest districts, with a simple Norman castle standing guard over the ancient ford at Latchford. A suspension bridge was constructed at Howley in 1911, linking the two banks of the Mersey. As the new housing estates at Westy grew up from the 1920s, this became a vital route for those working in Howley's industries.

Woolston, Padgate and Fearnhead

Woolston
Manchester Road, Paddington c1960 W29504
Paddington first emerged as a district in the mid 19th century as
the invention of a local soap manufacturer. By the 1950s, most
people associated it with the dreadful smell emerging from the
infamous bone works. Doubtless that would have been one
piece of Warrington's heritage which antiquarian Arthur Bennett
of Paddington House would not have been anxious to preserve!

Woolston, The Primary School, Hall Road c1955 W415017
This uncompromising modern building opened on 10 October 1952, and was soon filled with the post-war baby boom and the children of Woolston's new housing developments. Ancient Woolston Hall had once stood nearby; at the time of the Protestant Reformation, its occupants were staunchly Catholic.

Woolston, Hillock Lane c1955 W415008
By the 1950s there were still open fields near Hillock Lane as Woolston slowly began to develop from a farming community to a suburb of Warrington.

Woolston, Hillock Lane c1965 W415307
There are no smooth tarmac roads; few family cars dominate the gardens; there are no telephone poles, and above all no television aerials in this snapshot of post-war suburbia.

Padgate, Green Lane c1955 P271001
Over a century after Padgate was created as a separate parish in 1838, there is still an air of open countryside in this Green Lane. The opening on the left marked the entrance to Padgate Cottage Homes, built by the Board of Guardians in 1884 as an Industrial School. From 1930 to 1954 it served as a children's home.

◄ **Fearnhead, Station Road c1955** F135007
The Fearnhead post office on the corner of Fearnhead Lane (right) advertises Sanpic, which 'Destroys Sink Odours'. Soon the atmosphere of Fearnhead Cross itself would be destroyed with the redevelopment of the former RAF camp. The cobbled entry to the left would become Insall Road, named after a Group Captain Insall, former commander of the base.

Fearnhead, Bennett Recreation Ground c1955

F135001

This pleasant open space next to the railway line was donated as a recreation ground by Alderman Arthur Bennett, a former mayor and a passionate believer in the importance of preserving Warrington's historic and natural environment. Padgate's memorial obelisk to the 1914-18 war points to Padgate Camp, where millions of RAF recruits did their basic training between 1939-53.

Fearnhead Fearnhead Lane c1955

F135008

Time for a lunchtime pint at the Farmers Arms - but the owner of the bulbous Morris Minor on the forecourt had few drink-driving laws to worry about.

Woolston Long Barn Bridge c1965

W415002

Today the name Long Barn is associated with a modern housing development, but in 1965 the area was still open countryside and farmland. In 1968 Warrington was designated as a New Town, and a Development Corporation was created to create a 'prosperous dynamic town of opportunity and innovation'; new communities were built in the Padgate area, including Longbarn.

The Manchester Ship Canal

Thelwall, The Canal c1955
T328002
Laden with the products of Manchester's industries, a ship nears Latchford Locks at Thelwall. Begun in 1883, the Manchester Ship Canal was a major civil engineering project of the Victorian age. By its completion in December 1893, 17,000 'navvies' had shifted 54 million cubic yards of soil and rocks to create the 35.5-mile-long canal at the then staggering cost of £15 million. New sections of waterway were linked to the River Mersey to enable ocean-going vessels to reach the new inland port of Manchester and the neighbouring Lancashire cotton towns

**Latchford Locks
c1955** W29023
These are one of five
sets of locks used to
even out the water level
along the canal.
Latchford has parallel
locks; the larger one in
front of Richmond's'
works (left) measures
600 by 65 feet, taking a
large vessel and
tugboat. The sluice
gates behind the
smaller lock (right)
control the flow of
water and maintain a
constant level.

▼ **The Manchester Ship Canal c1960** W29057
After negotiating Latchford Locks, the 'Tarantia' from Glasgow passes under the 72ft 6in high Latchford railway viaduct, which was built to carry the London and North Western Railway line from Manchester via Stockport and Warrington to Liverpool.

▼ **The Knutsford Road Bridge c1955** W29010
Whilst the Latchford Viaduct is high enough to allow the tallest ships to pass beneath, a series of swing bridges allow vessels to pass through most road crossings along the canal. The 36-foot-wide Knutsford Road Bridge, near to Latchford Locks, rests on 60 rollers operated by hydraulic power to move its 248-foot length and 1,350 tons.

▲ **The Swing Bridge c1960** W29056
Manchester-bound, the 'Tarantia' passes through the Knutsford Road Swing Bridge towards Latchford Locks. A long way from his home port of Glasgow, the 'Tarantia's captain is escorted by a tugboat pilot more familiar with the difficult sections of the canal.

◄ **The High Level Bridge c1965** W29106
Known locally as 'The Cantilever', this high level fixed bridge provides a welcome escape route when the Knutsford and London Road swing bridges are closed. The Cantilever's design is similar to the high level bridge at Warburton, but fortunately for Warrington's frustrated motorists, no toll is exacted here!

◀ **Stockton Heath
The Ship Canal c1965**
S492001
A vessel passes close to
Walton Locks and
Warrington Wharf before
negotiating the Chester
Road Swing Bridge.
Originally, originally
Warrington's promoters
of the canal had ambitious
plans for a Warrington dock,
but this failed to materialise.
Walton Lock, however,
enabled vessels to leave
the canal and reach
Warrington's riverside
industries at Bank Quay and
unload at Bishop's Wharf.

◀ **The Manchester Ship Canal c1965** W29088
The 'Salford City' passes numerous stacks of imported timber at the yard in Station Road, Latchford. Timber was a major commodity carried on the canal; it was used not only by the building industry, but also in the manufacture of paper and cardboard, then a major Warrington industry.

◀ **The Manchester Ship Canal c1965** W29086
Having negotiated Latchford's locks, the viaduct and the swing bridge, the 'Salford City' moves on to close the bridge carrying the busy A49 London Road, which will cause chaos in Stockton Heath. As the volume of Warrington's road traffic increased, the constant stream of vessels on the canal brought unwelcome disruption to the local road network.

Around Lymm

Lymm, The Cross 1897 40483
In the distance a lone horseman rides into Lymm
village as it basks in the hot sunshine which has
compelled the draper, the ironmonger, and
Whitelegg the grocer to put up protective awnings
and blinds. It is the summer of Queen Victoria's
Diamond Jubilee year, but Lymm's celebrations are
not complete. To commemorate the sixtieth
anniversary of Queen Victoria's accession, Lymm
decided to restore the ancient cross, the
centrepiece of village life. The distinguished
architects Paley & Austin were commissioned to
reface the worn stone steps, fix more appropriate
finials and replace the cockerel with a symbolic
golden crown.

Lymm, The Bridge c1955 L122025

A delivery vehicle waits outside Henry Milling & Co's shop in this view from Lymm Cross towards the Bridgewater Canal. With the end of wartime rationing, the windows are stacked with groceries, perhaps to fight off competition from Burgons' opposite. Evans' family chemist's appears to be prescribing Whitbread's ale and stout, possibly available from the renamed Golden Fleece Hotel.

Lymm, The Dingle c1955 L122030

This view from The Groves shows The Cross (right) and Eagle Brow (left.) Today Martin's Bank (centre left) is occupied by an estate agent, reflecting Lymm's status as a housing hot spot, whilst Barclay's Bank (centre) trades from a less harmonious modern building. Nowadays the sound of birdsong and rushing water at The Dingle is likely to be drowned by impatient car horns!

Lymm, The Post Office c1950 L122003
Taken from the canal bridge, this photograph shows Bridgewater Street, looking towards Eagle Brow. Lymm post office, with the public telephone box outside, is on the left; on the right is the site of the present Saddler's Arms on the corner of Legh Street. The half-timbered facade of Martin's Bank can be seen in the distance.

Broomedge, The Post Office c1955 B560001
The post office and general store were essential parts of village life, so not surprisingly they feature on many of Frith's postcards; these were later sold at the post office counter and the village store! Meanwhile, the residents of Broomedge were being bombarded with adverts for Oxo - notice the advertising hoarding near the parked cars and the poster in the shop window.

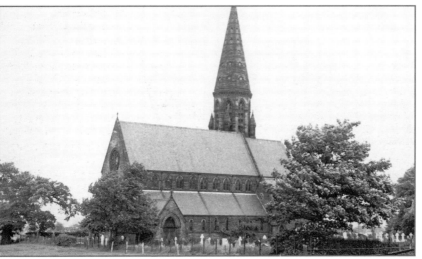

◀ **Oughtrington
The Church c1955** 089001
In 1862 George Charnley Dewhurst, a wealthy Manchester cotton magnate, bought the Oughtrington estates and became a benefactor to the village. He commissioned Slater and Carpenter of London to design St Peter's in the fashionable Gothic style at a cost of £10,000. He became the patron of the church, while Oughtrington became a separate parish from Lymm in 1881.

◄ **Broomedge
Burford Lane c1955**
B560003
It is hard to believe that this classic image of rural England was actually taken three years into the reign of Queen Elizabeth II and not at the beginning of the 20th century.

◄ **Warburton
The Old Church 1897**
39052
There had been a church dedicated to St Werburgh, daughter of the King of Mercia, at Warburton before the Normans. The church has been much altered; parts date back to the 14th century, with later additions from 1645 and 1711. In 1885 Rowland Egerton Warburton of Arley built a new church in the village.

◀ **High Legh
The Hall Chapel
c1955** H362005
The Legh family has had a long association with Lymm, and from the 13th century two branches of the family shared the manor of High Legh. This photograph shows the private chapel built in 1581 by the Leghs of East Legh Hall (later known as High Legh Hall.)

Lymm, The Church 1897 39084
This picturesque view shows the church of St Mary the Virgin from Lymm Dam. By 1850 an earlier 14th-century building was in disrepair, and the famous Newcastle architect John Dobson was commissioned to rebuild it. The 1521 tower was retained and raised, but the additional stonework proved too much for its foundations, and the tower was rebuilt in 1887.

▼ **High Legh, Swineyard Hall 1897** 40498
Formerly home to a branch of the Legh family, Swineyard Hall was sold off by Lt Colonel Cornwall Legh in 1919. The sale catalogue described it as a 'charming old-world residence, in black and white chequered design ... partially surrounded by a moat'; it was 'a comfortable and commodious domicile ... (with) interior fittings of rare old oak'.

Lymm, Arley Hall 1897 40496
This early Victorian mansion in Jacobean-revival style was built between 1833-45 on the site of an earlier house. The Nantwich architect George Latham found that his client, Rowland Egerton Warburton, demanded constant alterations to the design; this increased the cost from an original estimate of £5-6,000 to £30,000. The octagonal domed tower above the porch was removed in the alterations of 1968.

Thelwall, Grappenhall and Stockton Heath

Thelwall, The Pickering Arms c1955 T328005
Modern-day Warrington aspires to city status, but the Anglo-Saxon Chronicle records that the village of Thelwall briefly held that honour. 'In the year 923 (AD) King Edward the Elder founded a city here and called it Thelwall', proclaims the inscription on the gable end of the Pickering Arms (seen on the right of the photograph).

Thelwall, The Church 1897 40494
All Saints Church reflects the Victorian fashion for Gothic architecture. William Nicholson of Thelwall Hall financed its building in 1843 to replace an earlier chapel. All Saints is seen here after the addition of a chancel in 1857 and the alterations of the early 1890s. Its stained glass memorials to prominent Thelwall families include a window commemorating the Rylands, who were leading Warrington wire manufacturers.

Thelwall, The Village c1955 T328007
Today's motorists lane-hopping on the M6 over the nearby Thelwall viaduct might envy the traffic flow through 1950s Thelwall! The village's population has increased at least ten-fold in the intervening half century, but many of its historic buildings such as the Pickering Arms (right) have been preserved.

Thelwall, The Post Office c1955 T328004
The post office and the village shop were at the heart of Thelwall life in the mid 1950s. The public telephone box outside the post office reflects an era before mobile phones became commonplace, whilst the right-hand shop window of P L Greenway, 'grocer and provision dealer', is typical of the small general store which proceeded the supermarket age.

Grappenhall, The Village c1955 G200004
Grappenhall, or 'Gropenhale' (as it was then called), has the distinction of being recorded in the Domesday Survey of 1086. Bypassed by the Bridgewater canal, the cobbled village centre has retained much of its quaint atmosphere. Perhaps Frith's photographer sought refreshment at the imposing sandstone Ram's Head Hotel. Note the sundial set high above the door.

Grappenhall, The Canal c1955 G200005
The Bridgewater canal, built between 1759-1776, was a key transport network of the early Industrial Revolution, linking Manchester to Runcorn and carrying freight and passengers. The towpath on the right bank was used by the horses which once pulled the barges. Grappenhall has two of the characteristic narrow hump-backed bridges designed to carry road traffic over the canal.

Grappenhall, Church Street c1955 G200007
St Wilfrid's church has been central to Grappenhall life for almost 900 years. Although much modified over the centuries, it contains a font, parish chest and effigy of a knight from Norman times, and medieval stained glass. A stone carving on the tower might have inspired Lewis Carroll's Cheshire cat, as his father, the Reverend Dodgson, often visited St Wilfrid's.

Grappenhall, The Canal c1955 G200012
First railways and then the motor age signalled the end of the canal network for commercial use. Colourful pleasure craft and anglers now enjoy the tranquillity of the Bridgewater Canal as it passes through the south Warrington districts of Lymm, Thelwall, Grappenhall, Stockton Heath, Walton and Moore.

**Stockton Heath
Old London Road
c1965** S492008
Stockton Heath began
to develop as a
Warrington suburb with
the coming of the tram
in 1905. This view
towards the Ship Canal
shows London Road
free of today's endless
stream of traffic. The
left-hand side of the
street, beyond the tall
white facade of Robert's
shop, would soon
change dramatically
with the construction of
the Forge Shopping
Centre.

Walton, Daresbury and Moore

Walton
Walton Hall c1955 W29026

Begun in the mid 1830s, Walton Hall was to be both the family home and the country estate of Gilbert Greenall, a wealthy local brewer and prominent businessman. In the 1870s the hall was extended to accommodate the children of his second marriage and the enlarged household necessary now that he was Warrington's Member of Parliament and a baronet. By the death of Lord Daresbury, Sir Gilbert's son, in 1938, Walton had become a model agricultural estate. This view shows the original 1830s wing in Elizabethan style with its distinctive pinnacles (right), and the 1870s extension in Scottish baronial style (left).

Higher Walton, Walton Hall c1960 H526027
This view shows the visitor's entrance below the oriel window (left) and the single-storey gunroom next to it. The adjacent bay-windowed section contained the library below and Lady Daresbury's bedroom above. The three-storey wing (partially hidden by the tree) included the housekeeper's room and the butler's pantry. It was largely demolished in the late 1970s apart from the clock tower.

Walton, The Lily Pond, Walton Gardens c1955 W29053
Lady Daresbury took great pride in developing botanical gardens at Walton with specimen planting in the style of Kew; thousands of local people enjoyed visiting them on annual open days. In December 1941 Warrington Borough Council purchased the Hall and 171 surrounding acres from the Greenall family for £19,000. Since 1945, Walton Gardens have been a popular public park.

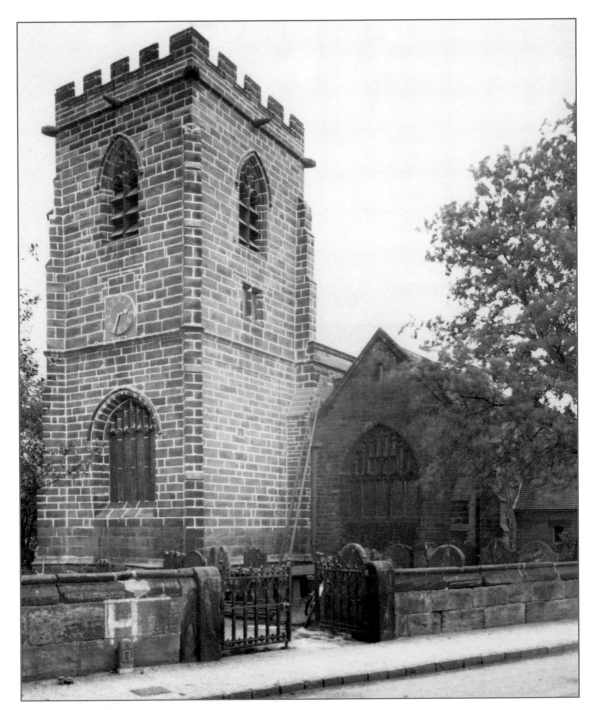

Daresbury, The Church c1955 D526032
One of All Saints' best-known features is the memorial window depicting characters from Lewis Carroll's 'Alice' stories. Lewis Carroll (his real name was Charles Lutwidge Dodgson) was born at Daresbury parsonage on 27 January 1832, and lived at Daresbury until 1843. Much of the present church dates from the rebuilding of the 1870s, financed by Sir Gilbert Greenall, Lord of the Manor of Daresbury. Gilbert's twin brother, Richard, was rector of Stretton, and sometimes preached at Daresbury in the Dodgsons' time. Perhaps Carroll was later inspired by the Greenall twins in his creation of look-alike brothers Tweedledum and Tweedledee.

Higher Walton, The Church c1960 H526032

St John's was designed by Paley and Austin, the distinguished Lancaster architects, and built in the local red sandstone by Fairhursts of Whitley. Consecrated in May 1885, the church was entirely financed by the first Sir Gilbert Greenall, a devout Anglican. St John's was the Greenall's family chapel, and Sir Gilbert, his son and grandson lie buried in its graveyard.

Moore
Greens Farm c1955 M240009

This timeless image of a black and white Cheshire farmhouse epitomised Moore's traditional agricultural character. In the half century since this photograph was taken, arable farming has been increasingly mechanised; like livestock farming, it has become less profitable. Sad to say, Greens Farm itself was demolished when part of the village was redeveloped.

▲ **Moore, The Post Office c1955** M240003 This deceptively simple photograph captures the spirit of Moore in 1955: the road curving out of the village; the essential Post Office; and an absence of menfolk, who were probably hard at work on the farms.

◄ **Moore, The Post Office c1955** M240004 Was this young Moore resident off to spend her pocket money at the local Post Office? Alas, there seems little there to tempt her, for the enamel advertising signs only offer Wills's Woodbine Cigarettes and Craven A tobacco, or seemingly saucy magazines such as Men Only and Tit Bits!

Moore, The School c1955 M240012
Moore's village school was showing its age in 1955. Built in 1877 for a much smaller community, its facilities had failed to keep pace with its teaching standards. An HMI's report of 1956 commented on the unsuitability of the cumbersome old school desks, the lack of dining facilities and the need for new toilets to replace 'the present bucket sanitation'.

Moore, The Canal Bridge c1955 M24008
A Moore resident keeps a look out for a rare commercial barge making its leisurely way along the Bridgewater Canal. Since this tranquil image was captured by Frith, only pleasure boats ply the canal and tie at up Moore to stock up at the village shop.

Index

Frith Book Co Titles

www.francisfrith.co.uk

The Frith Book Company publishes over 100 new titles each year. A selection of those currently available are listed below. For latest catalogue please contact Frith Book Co.

Town Books 96 pages, approx 100 photos. County and Themed Books 128 pages, approx 150 photos (unless specified). All titles hardback laminated case and jacket except those indicated pb (paperback)

Title	ISBN	Price	Title	ISBN	Price
Amersham, Chesham & Rickmansworth (pb)			Derby (pb)	1-85937-367-4	£9.99
	1-85937-340-2	£9.99	Derbyshire (pb)	1-85937-196-5	£9.99
Ancient Monuments & Stone Circles	1-85937-143-4	£17.99	Devon (pb)	1-85937-297-x	£9.99
Aylesbury (pb)	1-85937-227-9	£9.99	Dorset (pb)	1-85937-269-4	£9.99
Bakewell	1-85937-113-2	£12.99	Dorset Churches	1-85937-172-8	£17.99
Barnstaple (pb)	1-85937-300-3	£9.99	Dorset Coast (pb)	1-85937-299-6	£9.99
Bath (pb)	1-85937419-0	£9.99	Dorset Living Memories	1-85937-210-4	£14.99
Bedford (pb)	1-85937-205-8	£9.99	Down the Severn	1-85937-118-3	£14.99
Berkshire (pb)	1-85937-191-4	£9.99	Down the Thames (pb)	1-85937-278-3	£9.99
Berkshire Churches	1-85937-170-1	£17.99	Down the Trent	1-85937-311-9	£14.99
Blackpool (pb)	1-85937-382-8	£9.99	Dublin (pb)	1-85937-231-7	£9.99
Bognor Regis (pb)	1-85937-431-x	£9.99	East Anglia (pb)	1-85937-265-1	£9.99
Bournemouth	1-85937-067-5	£12.99	East London	1-85937-080-2	£14.99
Bradford (pb)	1-85937-204-x	£9.99	East Sussex	1-85937-130-2	£14.99
Brighton & Hove(pb)	1-85937-192-2	£8.99	Eastbourne	1-85937-061-6	£12.99
Bristol (pb)	1-85937-264-3	£9.99	Edinburgh (pb)	1-85937-193-0	£8.99
British Life A Century Ago (pb)	1-85937-213-9	£9.99	England in the 1880s	1-85937-331-3	£17.99
Buckinghamshire (pb)	1-85937-200-7	£9.99	English Castles (pb)	1-85937-434-4	£9.99
Camberley (pb)	1-85937-222-8	£9.99	English Country Houses	1-85937-161-2	£17.99
Cambridge (pb)	1-85937-422-0	£9.99	Essex (pb)	1-85937-270-8	£9.99
Cambridgeshire (pb)	1-85937-420-4	£9.99	Exeter	1-85937-126-4	£12.99
Canals & Waterways (pb)	1-85937-291-0	£9.99	Exmoor	1-85937-132-9	£14.99
Canterbury Cathedral (pb)	1-85937-179-5	£9.99	Falmouth	1-85937-066-7	£12.99
Cardiff (pb)	1-85937-093-4	£9.99	Folkestone (pb)	1-85937-124-8	£9.99
Carmarthenshire	1-85937-216-3	£14.99	Glasgow (pb)	1-85937-190-6	£9.99
Chelmsford (pb)	1-85937-310-0	£9.99	Gloucestershire	1-85937-102-7	£14.99
Cheltenham (pb)	1-85937-095-0	£9.99	Great Yarmouth (pb)	1-85937-426-3	£9.99
Cheshire (pb)	1-85937-271-6	£9.99	Greater Manchester (pb)	1-85937-266-x	£9.99
Chester	1-85937-090-x	£12.99	Guildford (pb)	1-85937-410-7	£9.99
Chesterfield	1-85937-378-x	£9.99	Hampshire (pb)	1-85937-279-1	£9.99
Chichester (pb)	1-85937-228-7	£9.99	Hampshire Churches (pb)	1-85937-207-4	£9.99
Colchester (pb)	1-85937-188-4	£8.99	Harrogate	1-85937-423-9	£9.99
Cornish Coast	1-85937-163-9	£14.99	Hastings & Bexhill (pb)	1-85937-131-0	£9.99
Cornwall (pb)	1-85937-229-5	£9.99	Heart of Lancashire (pb)	1-85937-197-3	£9.99
Cornwall Living Memories	1-85937-248-1	£14.99	Helston (pb)	1-85937-214-7	£9.99
Cotswolds (pb)	1-85937-230-9	£9.99	Hereford (pb)	1-85937-175-2	£9.99
Cotswolds Living Memories	1-85937-255-4	£14.99	Herefordshire	1-85937-174-4	£14.99
County Durham	1-85937-123-x	£14.99	Hertfordshire (pb)	1-85937-247-3	£9.99
Croydon Living Memories	1-85937-162-0	£9.99	Horsham (pb)	1-85937-432-8	£9.99
Cumbria	1-85937-101-9	£14.99	Humberside	1-85937-215-5	£14.99
Dartmoor	1-85937-145-0	£14.99	Hythe, Romney Marsh & Ashford	1-85937-256-2	£9.99

Available from your local bookshop or from the publisher

Frith Book Co Titles (continued)

Title	ISBN	Price	Title	ISBN	Price
Ipswich (pb)	1-85937-424-7	£9.99	St Ives (pb)	1-85937415-8	£9.99
Ireland (pb)	1-85937-181-7	£9.99	Scotland (pb)	1-85937-182-5	£9.99
Isle of Man (pb)	1-85937-268-6	£9.99	Scottish Castles (pb)	1-85937-323-2	£9.99
Isles of Scilly	1-85937-136-1	£14.99	Sevenoaks & Tunbridge	1-85937-057-8	£12.99
Isle of Wight (pb)	1-85937-429-8	£9.99	Sheffield, South Yorks (pb)	1-85937-267-8	£9.99
Isle of Wight Living Memories	1-85937-304-6	£14.99	Shrewsbury (pb)	1-85937-325-9	£9.99
Kent (pb)	1-85937-189-2	£9.99	Shropshire (pb)	1-85937-326-7	£9.99
Kent Living Memories	1-85937-125-6	£14.99	Somerset	1-85937-153-1	£14.99
Lake District (pb)	1-85937-275-9	£9.99	South Devon Coast	1-85937-107-8	£14.99
Lancaster, Morecambe & Heysham (pb)	1-85937-233-3	£9.99	South Devon Living Memories	1-85937-168-x	£14.99
Leeds (pb)	1-85937-202-3	£9.99	South Hams	1-85937-220-1	£14.99
Leicester	1-85937-073-x	£12.99	Southampton (pb)	1-85937-427-1	£9.99
Leicestershire (pb)	1-85937-185-x	£9.99	Southport (pb)	1-85937-425-5	£9.99
Lincolnshire (pb)	1-85937-433-6	£9.99	Staffordshire	1-85937-047-0	£12.99
Liverpool & Merseyside (pb)	1-85937-234-1	£9.99	Stratford upon Avon	1-85937-098-5	£12.99
London (pb)	1-85937-183-3	£9.99	Suffolk (pb)	1-85937-221-x	£9.99
Ludlow (pb)	1-85937-176-0	£9.99	Suffolk Coast	1-85937-259-7	£14.99
Luton (pb)	1-85937-235-x	£9.99	Surrey (pb)	1-85937-240-6	£9.99
Maidstone	1-85937-056-x	£14.99	Sussex (pb)	1-85937-184-1	£9.99
Manchester (pb)	1-85937-198-1	£9.99	Swansea (pb)	1-85937-167-1	£9.99
Middlesex	1-85937-158-2	£14.99	Tees Valley & Cleveland	1-85937-211-2	£14.99
New Forest	1-85937-128-0	£14.99	Thanet (pb)	1-85937-116-7	£9.99
Newark (pb)	1-85937-366-6	£9.99	Tiverton (pb)	1-85937-178-7	£9.99
Newport, Wales (pb)	1-85937-258-9	£9.99	Torbay	1-85937-063-2	£12.99
Newquay (pb)	1-85937-421-2	£9.99	Truro	1-85937-147-7	£12.99
Norfolk (pb)	1-85937-195-7	£9.99	Victorian and Edwardian Cornwall	1-85937-252-x	£14.99
Norfolk Living Memories	1-85937-217-1	£14.99	Victorian & Edwardian Devon	1-85937-253-8	£14.99
Northamptonshire	1-85937-150-7	£14.99	Victorian & Edwardian Kent	1-85937-149-3	£14.99
Northumberland Tyne & Wear (pb)	1-85937-281-3	£9.99	Vic & Ed Maritime Album	1-85937-144-2	£17.99
North Devon Coast	1-85937-146-9	£14.99	Victorian and Edwardian Sussex	1-85937-157-4	£14.99
North Devon Living Memories	1-85937-261-9	£14.99	Victorian & Edwardian Yorkshire	1-85937-154-x	£14.99
North London	1-85937-206-6	£14.99	Victorian Seaside	1-85937-159-0	£17.99
North Wales (pb)	1-85937-298-8	£9.99	Villages of Devon (pb)	1-85937-293-7	£9.99
North Yorkshire (pb)	1-85937-236-8	£9.99	Villages of Kent (pb)	1-85937-294-5	£9.99
Norwich (pb)	1-85937-194-9	£8.99	Villages of Sussex (pb)	1-85937-295-3	£9.99
Nottingham (pb)	1-85937-324-0	£9.99	Warwickshire (pb)	1-85937-203-1	£9.99
Nottinghamshire (pb)	1-85937-187-6	£9.99	Welsh Castles (pb)	1-85937-322-4	£9.99
Oxford (pb)	1-85937-411-5	£9.99	West Midlands (pb)	1-85937-289-9	£9.99
Oxfordshire (pb)	1-85937-430-1	£9.99	West Sussex	1-85937-148-5	£14.99
Peak District (pb)	1-85937-280-5	£9.99	West Yorkshire (pb)	1-85937-201-5	£9.99
Penzance	1-85937-069-1	£12.99	Weymouth (pb)	1-85937-209-0	£9.99
Peterborough (pb)	1-85937-219-8	£9.99	Wiltshire (pb)	1-85937-277-5	£9.99
Piers	1-85937-237-6	£17.99	Wiltshire Churches (pb)	1-85937-171-x	£9.99
Plymouth	1-85937-119-1	£12.99	Wiltshire Living Memories	1-85937-245-7	£14.99
Poole & Sandbanks (pb)	1-85937-251-1	£9.99	Winchester (pb)	1-85937-428-x	£9.99
Preston (pb)	1-85937-212-0	£9.99	Windmills & Watermills	1-85937-242-2	£17.99
Reading (pb)	1-85937-238-4	£9.99	Worcester (pb)	1-85937-165-5	£9.99
Romford (pb)	1-85937-319-4	£9.99	Worcestershire	1-85937-152-3	£14.99
Salisbury (pb)	1-85937-239-2	£9.99	York (pb)	1-85937-199-x	£9.99
Scarborough (pb)	1-85937-379-8	£9.99	Yorkshire (pb)	1-85937-186-8	£9.99
St Albans (pb)	1-85937-341-0	£9.99	Yorkshire Living Memories	1-85937-166-3	£14.99

See Frith books on the internet www.francisfrith.co.uk

FRITH PRODUCTS & SERVICES

Francis Frith would doubtless be pleased to know that the pioneering publishing venture he started in 1860 still continues today. A hundred and forty years later, The Francis Frith Collection continues in the same innovative tradition and is now one of the foremost publishers of vintage photographs in the world. Some of the current activities include:

Interior Decoration

Today Frith's photographs can be seen framed and as giant wall murals in thousands of pubs, restaurants, hotels, banks, retail stores and other public buildings throughout the country. In every case they enhance the unique local atmosphere of the places they depict and provide reminders of gentler days in an increasingly busy and frenetic world.

Product Promotions

Frith products are used by many major companies to promote the sales of their own products or to reinforce their own history and heritage. Frith promotions have been used by Hovis bread, Courage beers, Scots Porage Oats, Colman's mustard, Cadbury's foods, Mellow Birds coffee, Dunhill pipe tobacco, Guinness, and Bulmer's Cider.

Genealogy and Family History

As the interest in family history and roots grows world-wide, more and more people are turning to Frith's photographs of Great Britain for images of the towns, villages and streets where their ancestors lived; and, of course, photographs of the churches and chapels where their ancestors were christened, married and buried are an essential part of every genealogy tree and family album.

Frith Products

All Frith photographs are available Framed or just as Mounted Prints and Posters (size 23 x 16 inches). These may be ordered from the address below. From time to time other products - Address Books, Calendars, Table Mats, etc - are available.

The Internet

Already twenty thousand Frith photographs can be viewed and purchased on the internet through the Frith websites and a myriad of partner sites.

For more detailed information on Frith companies and products, look at these sites:

www.francisfrith.co.uk
www.francisfrith.com
(for North American visitors)

See the complete list of Frith Books at:

www.francisfrith.co.uk

This web site is regularly updated with the latest list of publications from the Frith Book Company. If you wish to buy books relating to another part of the country that your local bookshop does not stock, you may purchase on-line.

For further information, trade, or author enquiries please contact us at the address below:
The Francis Frith Collection, Frith's Barn, Teffont, Salisbury, Wiltshire, England SP3 5QP.
Tel: +44 (0)1722 716 376 Fax: +44 (0)1722 716 881 Email: sales@francisfrith.co.uk

---

See Frith books on the internet www.francisfrith.co.uk

TO RECEIVE YOUR FREE MOUNTED PRINT

Mounted Print
Overall size 14 x 11 inches

Cut out this Voucher and return it with your remittance for £1.95 to cover postage and handling, to UK addresses. For overseas addresses please include £4.00 post and handling. Choose any photograph included in this book. Your SEPIA print will be A4 in size, and mounted in a cream mount with burgundy rule line, overall size 14 x 11 inches.

Order additional Mounted Prints at HALF PRICE (only £7.49 each*)

If there are further pictures you would like to order, possibly as gifts for friends and family, purchase them at half price (no additional postage and handling required).

Have your Mounted Prints framed*

For an additional £14.95 per print you can have your chosen Mounted Print framed in an elegant polished wood and gilt moulding, overall size 16 x 13 inches (no additional postage and handling required).

---
* IMPORTANT!
These special prices are only available if ordered using the original voucher on this page (no copies permitted) and at the same time as your free Mounted Print, for delivery to the same address
---

Frith Collectors' Guild

From time to time we publish a magazine of news and stories about Frith photographs and further special offers of Frith products. If you would like 12 months FREE membership, please return this form.

Send completed forms to:
The Francis Frith Collection, Frith's Barn, Teffont, Salisbury, Wiltshire SP3 5QP

Voucher for **FREE** and Reduced Price Frith Prints

Picture no.	Page number	Qty	Mounted @ £7.49	Framed + £14.95	Total Cost
		1	**Free of charge***	£	£
			£7.49	£	£
			£7.49	£	£
			£7.49	£	£
			£7.49	£	£
			£7.49	£	£

Please allow 28 days for delivery   *** Post & handling** £1.95

Book Title . . . .   **Total Order Cost** £

Please do not photocopy this voucher. Only the original is valid, so please cut it out and return it to us.

I enclose a cheque / postal order for £ . . . .
made payable to 'The Francis Frith Collection'
OR please debit my Mastercard / Visa / Switch / Amex card
(credit cards please on all overseas orders)

Number . . . .

Issue No(Switch only) . . . . .Valid from (Amex/Switch) . . . .

Expires . . . . Signature . . . .

Name Mr/Mrs/Ms . . . .

Address . . . .

. . . .

. . . . Postcode . . . .

Daytime Tel No . . . .   Valid to 31/12/03

The Francis Frith Collectors' Guild
Please enrol me as a member for 12 months free of charge.

Name Mr/Mrs/Ms . . . .

Address . . . .

. . . .

. . . . Postcode . . . .

Would you like to find out more about Francis Frith?

We have recently recruited some entertaining speakers who are happy to visit local groups, clubs and societies to give an illustrated talk documenting Frith's travels and photographs. If you are a member of such a group and are interested in hosting a presentation, we would love to hear from you.

Our speakers bring with them a small selection of our local town and county books, together with sample prints. They are happy to take orders. A small proportion of the order value is donated to the group who have hosted the presentation. The talks are therefore an excellent way of fundraising for small groups and societies.

Can you help us with information about any of the Frith photographs in this book?

We are gradually compiling an historical record for each of the photographs in the Frith archive. It is always fascinating to find out the names of the people shown in the pictures, as well as insights into the shops, buildings and other features depicted.

If you recognize anyone in the photographs in this book, or if you have information not already included in the author's caption, do let us know. We would love to hear from you, and will try to publish it in future books or articles.

Our production team

Frith books are produced by a small dedicated team at offices in the converted Grade II listed 18th-century barn at Teffont near Salisbury, illustrated above. Most have worked with the Frith Collection for many years. All have in common one quality: they have a passion for the Frith Collection. The team is constantly expanding, but currently includes:

Jason Buck, John Buck, Douglas Burns, Heather Crisp, Lucy Elcock, Isobel Hall, Rob Hames, Hazel Heaton, Peter Horne, James Kinnear, Tina Leary, Hannah Marsh, Eliza Sackett, Terence Sackett, Sandra Sanger, Lewis Taylor, Shelley Tolcher, Helen Vimpany, Clive Wathen and Jenny Wathen.

Free Print – see overleaf